Sammie and Sue
The Rescue

Book 1

Susan McLain

ISBN 979-8-89309-336-0 (Paperback)
ISBN 979-8-89309-337-7 (Digital)

Covenant Books
11661 Hwy 707
Murrells Inlet, SC 29576
www.covenantbooks.com

Book theme: God sent Jesus to rescue us.

For the Son of Man came to seek and save those who are lost.

—Luke 19:10

Sammie and Sue were pals from day one. Sammie, an Aussie rescue pup, was so much fun!

Sue was just seven when she first met the pup. Sammie walked right over and drank from her cup.

From there, she soon sat right in her lap and then went on to take a short little nap.

Sue laughed and she giggled a moment or so, then tried to give her kisses to just say hello.

Sue hated to wake her since she had just fallen asleep, but Mom was calling her in to go eat.

So Sue got up slowly, and Sammie followed her in, then with a wet, growly shake to begin.

A low, little growl like she had something to say, and so Sue found a small toy to play.

And after Sue ate, it was Sammie's turn now. The food went into the bowl, then it turned over somehow.

All over the floor, the food lay like a maze. Sue laughed and she giggled! Sue sat there amazed!

They sat on the floor playing a moment or two, then oh no, a wet spot, and out the door they flew.

Out playing in the sun, Sue and her pup, running and rolling in the grass and stuff.

Sammie made a small little bark and ran some more, then the chocolate Lab, Brady, came by from next door.

So Brady came over to Sammie to smell her; she didn't like it one bit and wanted Sue to protect her.

Sue picked up her pup as Mom and Dad were watching, just to make sure Brady was nice and not barking.

They smelled each other for a moment or two, and then Brady went home as Sammie barked at him too.

i love Sammie

The day ended nicely with a bath in the tub, with soap mustaches and a soft tan coat to scrub.

i love Sa

Then Sammie jumped up and the water it went, all down the side, right into the floor vent.

17

So, grabbing a big, fluffy towel or two, they bundled together, Sammie and Sue.

A quick story as they both went to bed, and Sammie laid down with her soft, wet head.

Sue kissed her goodnight on her forehead and said, "Sleep tight, dear Sammie, enjoy your bed.

God loves us, you know. He brought us together now we can be together forever.

So, thank You, God, for this pretty new pup; help me take care of her and such.

Just like You do for me, dear God, for loving me, saving me, it's all so much.

All glory and praises again, in Jesus's name we pray, Amen."

Hello
Kitty

Then Mom and Dad checked in on those two, Sue on the floor, both quite a snooze!

With Sue's hand through the crate, holding a paw or a foot, they praised God together, for they knew she was hooked.

The love they all shared, it could fill the room; together the four, love was abloom!

And as they lay there together, Sammie and Sue, the two dreaming of all the new things they would do!

For my little friends:

For the Son of Man came to seek and save
those who are lost. (Luke 19:10)

God sent Jesus to rescue us! What does this Bible verse mean? Well, when Jesus came to earth as a baby, born in Bethlehem, although He remained God, He also became man. God loved us so much, He sent Jesus, His one and only Son, to Earth to rescue us and save us from our sins. God wants to show us how we can get to Heaven. We can get to Heaven by *ac*cepting Jesus as our Savior, by *be*lieving Jesus is the Son of God, and by *c*onfessing our sins (all the bad things we say and do and think) to Jesus. Remember it this way: ABC (accept, believe, confess). Pour out your heart to Jesus in prayer. He loves you!

For parents: We parents must work diligently to keep open those lines of communication, especially with our older kids during these crazy, confusing times in which we live; sharing with them that there is always hope, forgiveness, and everlasting love through Jesus. Letting them know, without any doubt, that there is never any insurmountable issue that we can't handle together. That they are loved unconditionally. That we have their back—no matter what! That's what God does for us! That God has it all planned out—He even factored in our stupidity—and that because He loves us so much, there is that "rescue plan," fulfilled in our dear Lord, Jesus Christ our Savior! Thank You, God, our Father!

About the Author

Addie and Libby

Born into a military family and raised in a small, patriotic town in Northwest Florida, Susan attended Florida State University and graduated with an art degree. Dreams of working at Disney World were put on hold as she met her husband, Mike, and they settled down in the same town she grew up in. They raised two beautiful daughters and lots of dogs! Susan worked as an illustrator for several defense contractors, but the job she loved the most, after being a stay-at-home mom for years, was that of Children's Director at a local church. She loves to write Bible-based curriculum for Sunday school and summer camp and loves teaching kids about Christ.